First World War
and Army of Occupation
War Diary
France, Belgium and Germany

37 DIVISION
Divisional Troops
Royal Army Medical Corps
Divisional Field Ambulance Workshop Unit
1 August 1915 - 31 March 1916

WO95/2526/2

The Naval & Military Press Ltd
www.nmarchive.com
Published in association with The National Archives

Published by

The Naval & Military Press Ltd

Unit 10 Ridgewood Industrial Park,

Uckfield, East Sussex,

TN22 5QE England

Tel: +44 (0) 1825 749494

www.naval-military-press.com

www.nmarchive.com

This diary has been reprinted in facsimile from the original. Any imperfections are inevitably reproduced and the quality may fall short of modern type and cartographic standards.

© **Crown Copyright**
Images reproduced by permission of The National Archives, London, England, 2015.

Contents

Document type	Place/Title	Date From	Date To
Heading	WO95/2526/2 1915 Aug-1916 Mar 37 Div Field Amb W/shop Unit		
Heading	37th Division Medical. 37th Fd Amb W'shop Unit Aug 1915-Mar 1916		
Heading	37th Divn. 37 Divn Field Amb Workshop Unit Vol I & II Aug 15 Sept 15		
Heading	War Diary 37 Division. Field Ambulance Workshop Unit		
War Diary	Neufchatel	01/08/1915	01/08/1915
War Diary	Abbeville	02/08/1915	02/08/1915
War Diary	Moulle	03/08/1915	03/08/1915
War Diary	Eeke	04/08/1915	04/08/1915
War Diary	Hazebrouck	05/08/1915	26/08/1915
War Diary	Doullens	27/08/1915	31/08/1915
Heading	August 1915 37th Div F.A.W.U. O.C Mackay Lieut (Volume 1)		
War Diary	Rouen	01/08/1915	01/08/1915
War Diary	Neufchatel	02/08/1915	02/08/1915
War Diary	Abbeville	03/08/1915	03/08/1915
War Diary	Moulle	04/08/1915	04/08/1915
War Diary	Eecke	05/08/1915	05/08/1915
War Diary	Hazebroock	06/08/1915	26/08/1915
War Diary	Doullens	27/08/1915	31/08/1915
Heading	September 1915 37th Div. F.A.W.U. O.C. Mackay 2 Lieut.		
War Diary	Doullens	01/09/1915	05/09/1915
War Diary	Pas	06/09/1915	30/09/1915
Heading	37th Division 37th Divl. F.A.W. Unit Oct 15 Vol 3		
Heading	October 1915 37th Div F.A.W.U. O.C Mackay Lieut. Volume 3		
War Diary	Pas	01/10/1915	31/10/1915
Heading	37th Division. 37th F.A.W.U. Vol 4 Nov 15		
Heading	War Diary Of A.C. Mackay 2nd Lieut Commanding 37th Div. F.A.W.U. From 1st Nov. 1915 To 30th Nov. 1915 Volume 4		
War Diary Miscellaneous	Pas	01/11/1915	30/11/1915
Heading	37th Division. 37th F.A.W.U. Vol 5 December 1915		
Heading	Of 2 Lieut. A.C. Mackay O/C 37th Div. F.A.W.U. Dec 1915 Volume V		
War Diary	Pas	01/12/1915	31/12/1915
Heading	37th F.A.W.U. Vol 6 Jan 16		
Heading	Of Lieut A.G. Mackay O/C 37th Div F.A.W.U. For January 1916 (Volume 6)		
War Diary	Pas	01/01/1916	31/01/1916
Heading	37th F.A.W.U. Feb 1916		
Heading	37th F.A.W.U. Vol. 7		
Heading	Of Lieut A.C. Mackay O/C 37th Div F.A.W.U. February 1916 Volume 7		
War Diary	Pas	01/02/1916	19/02/1916

War Diary	Bavincourt	20/02/1916	29/02/1916
Heading	37th Div F.A.W.U Vol 8 March 1916		
Heading	Of Lieut A.C. Mackay O/C 37th Div F.A.W.U. March 1916 Volume 8		
War Diary	Bavincourt	01/03/1916	19/03/1916
War Diary	Luchieux	20/03/1916	31/03/1916

WO 95 2526/2

1915 AUG - 1916 MAY
37 DIV FIELD AMB WKSHOP UNIT

37TH DIVISION
MEDICAL

37TH FD AMB W'SHOP UNIT
AUG 1915 - MAR 1916

37/15 WD

34th Divl. Field Amb. Workshop Unit.

Vols I & II

121/7198

mys

Aug. } 1915
Sept. }

Aug 15
Sept 15
Nov. 16

War Diary

37th Division
Field Ambulance Workshop Unit

August

O.C. Mackay
Lieut

Army Form C. 2118

WAR DIARY

~~INTELLIGENCE SUMMARY~~

(Erase heading not required.)

Instructions regarding War Diaries and Intelligence Summaries are contained in F. S. Regs., Part II. and the Staff Manual respectively. Title Pages will be prepared in manuscript.

37" Div 74 Ant. Workshop

Place	Date	Hour	Summary of Events and Information	Remarks and references to Appendices
Neufchatel	1/8/15	9 p.m.	Drew money at Rouen, paid men. Rep'r Rover with Ambulance Car and Workshop trailer & arrived without incident at Neufchatel.	O.C.M.
Attagnies	2/8/15	11 p.m.	Reveille 5 a.m. Rep'r Neufchatel at 6.30 a.m. After passing Hesdin .? went on in advance to Attagnies, reported to Base Commander. Ord'rs arrived. Sent for men, also reported to A.D.J.T. Returned & picked up Steam - Parkes team in carr't. On inspection found Tyre stuffing on Peerless Workshop, attempted to exchange wheel with another Peerless or advance M.T. Bos tur, as wheels would not interchange.	O.C.M
Moulle	3/8/15	12 p.m.	Reveille 5 a.m. Rep'r Attagnies at 7 a.m. Ford overheats on long hill. Outside Fruges Peerless Workshop Tyre strips(?). Letter sent(?) convoy on to Fruges. Telephoned D.J.T. re breakdown gave which arrived at 6 p.m. Took convoy on to Moulle except Workshop which went to St. Omer. 37" Div Rep'rs went to St. Omer. Reported H.Q.O.C. Troops, ordered to Renescure early morning in order.	O.C.M

1875 Wt. W593/826 1,000,000 4/15 J.B.C. & A. A.D.S.S./Forms/C. 2118.

Army Form C. 2118

WAR DIARY
INTELLIGENCE SUMMARY
(Erase heading not required.)

Instructions regarding War Diaries and Intelligence Summaries are contained in F. S. Regs., Part II. and the Staff Manual respectively. Title Pages will be prepared in manuscript.

Place	Date	Hour	Summary of Events and Information	Remarks and references to Appendices
Eecke	4/8/15	10 p.m.	Reveille 4 A.M. Reported to 37 Div. D.A.Q.M.G. at Renescure who promised to send orders later. Drew petrol & rations at S.V. & made a collection of Watch strap. Ambulance cars thoroughly cleaned. No orders received so returned Div. to Hazebrouck. Went on to Caestre (Div. H.Q.) & 5 orders to allot Ambulance Cars to 5 Fd. Am. Brigades & sub divs. to allot 50 Fd. Am. at Hazebrouck, 7 cars at 49 Fd. Am. heavy 7 cars at 50 Fd. Am. at 48 Fd. Am. at Eecke. R.V. at St. Sylvestre & 7 cars at 48 Fd. Am. at Eecke. R.V. Workshop. Men temporarily in a yard.	O.C. M.
Hazebrouck	5/8/15	8 p.m.	Joined 48 Fd. Am. but found road & farm unsuitable for heavy workshops. Found a convenient yard in Hazebrouck - more than cars inspected by A.D.M.S. for Motor Amb. Convoy & given a lorry & orders for structural alterations.	O.C. M.
Hazebrouck	6/8/15	6 p.m.	Reveille 6 a.m. Commenced alterations to Workshop Mot. Car. Went to Caestre and saw the D.A.D.O.S. to write for service pair.	O.C. M.
Hazebrouck	7/8/15	6 p.m.	Reveille 6 a.m. Inspected 50 & 49 Fd. Am. cars for deficiencies & their pumps & covers & for Whitley & goods to send in for alterations. allotted 1 Whitley & 3 Fords.	O.C. M.

1875 Wt. W593/826 1,000,000 4/15 J.B.C. & A. A.D.S.S./Forms/C.2118.

Army Form C. 2118

WAR DIARY

~~INTELLIGENCE SUMMARY~~

(Erase heading not required.)

Instructions regarding War Diaries and Intelligence Summaries are contained in F.S. Regs, Part II. and the Staff Manual respectively. Title Pages will be prepared in manuscript.

Place	Date	Hour	Summary of Events and Information	Remarks and references to Appendices
Hazebrouck	8/8/15	6 p.m.	Reveillé 6 a.m. Inspected 1st & 8th Cav. Bde for changes in cars. Arranged w Staff Capt. to come for alterations. Officers in Staff Cars. Arranged to put mail cars on Radmed	ACM
Hazebrouck	9/8/15	6 p.m.	Reveillé 6 A.M. continued structural repairs to Amb Cars. Went to Isbergues + purchased fittings for lavatories. Spares 3.3 p.r. Went to Isbergues to find the file free. Ordered workshop wheel to be made to the morrow.	ACM
Hazebrouck	10/8/15	6 p.m.	Reveillé 6 A.M. Continued structural alterations, par workshop lorry wheel re-tyred at Isbergues. Repaired Triumph motor cycle & handed over to despatch rider Section	ACM
Hazebrouck	11/8/15	6 p.m.	Reveillé 6 A.M. Repaired Leo Ford car, also dress indents for Calcium windows for Ford Repairs & Headlights & continued alterations to Cars.	ACM
Hazebrouck	12/8/15	6 p.m.	Reveillé 6 A.M. Inspected all ambulance cars & fixed speed limit 15 mph. Ford 15 repair, smashed Radiator Headpipes. Reduced Corporal for driving car smashed Ford. Made note this for 37 Div. Supply Col. Repaired Douglas bike	ACM
Hazebrouck	13/8/15	6 p.m.	Reveillé 6 A.M. Went to Div. H.Q. - handed in returns etc. Ford repairs - finished - returns to Section. Continued alterations to	ACM

WAR DIARY

~~INTELLIGENCE SUMMARY~~

(Erase heading not required.)

Army Form C. 2118

Instructions regarding War Diaries and Intelligence Summaries are contained in F. S. Regs., Part II. and the Staff Manual respectively. Title Pages will be prepared in manuscript.

Place	Date	Hour	Summary of Events and Information	Remarks and references to Appendices
Hazebrouck	15/8/15	6 p.m.	Reveille 6 A.M. Went to Aubyville to enquire into a very urgent case which allowed to witness special antonio's sport incidents. Returned too tired to water lorry. Made a note for Watson to settle.	Capt.
Hazebrouck	16/8/15	6 p.m.	Reveille 6 A.M. Ford smashed, broken chassis connecting rod. Head lights etc. Went to Balham & found letter for Cornelius and paid 27. Had to hurry on car to supply lorry to get to Watson.	A.C.M.
Hazebrouck	17/8/15	6 p.m.	Reveille 6 A.M. Inspected amb. cars at its Section. Toured in No 2 W/Shop with Rees showed M'war huts. Wind for autobus. Received complaint their W/shop tents were late their full load decided to straighten spring.	A.C.M.
Hazebrouck	18/8/15	6 p.m.	Reveille 6 A.M. & even more ideas in the helmets from D.A.D.O.S. Brought back paint for Amb. Cars. Went to Div. H.Q.	A.C.M.
Hazebrouck	19/8/15	6 p.m.	Reveille 6 A.M. Started paint out. Car service sto. Went to Steenwerke - brought spring lead paid 7.50 frs. Tempered & continued spring steel.	A.C.M.
Hazebrouck	20/8/15	6 p.m.	Reveille 6 A.M. Took down rear spring of NO 19 W/Shop to get fitted extra leaf. Paint 6 cars, also identification markets.	A.C.M.

WAR DIARY

INTELLIGENCE SUMMARY

Army Form C. 2118

Instructions regarding War Diaries and Intelligence Summaries are contained in F.S. Regs., Part II. and the Staff Manual respectively. Title Pages will be prepared in manuscript.

(Erase heading not required.)

Place	Date	Hour	Summary of Events and Information	Remarks and references to Appendices
Hazebrouck	21/8/15	6 p.m.	Reveille 6 A.M. Finished spring, refitted & took out for test. Found axle is could be carried, installed & 2 × steel horn & timer cleaned. Wdconied to lorries.	a.e.m
Hazebrouck	22/8/15	6 p.m.	Reveille 6 A.M. Started on ten springs. 2 send as W. Shelay. Went to Steinbeck - Insegen steel springs for car pair 38 fr. Made a ? & wooden packer for car O.C. 37 Div. Inspected munitions of 51st W. Shelay.	a.e.m
Hazebrouck	23/8/15	6 p.m.	Reveille 6 A.M. Drew white paint from D.A.D.O.S. started fairs. Finished painting all Amb. Cars.	a.e.m
Hazebrouck	24/8/15	6 p.m.	Reveille 6 A.M. Inspected another W. Shelay, repaired Ford. Mended magneto of W.O.2 Shelay, repaired Ford. 2 Douglas in 27". Received orders for movement to Doullens.	a.e.m
Hazebrouck	25/8/15	6 p.m.	Reveille 6 A.M. Finished springs, 100 sets W. Shelays. Repaired Ford springs, found out new adjustm.	a.e.m
Hazebrouck	26/8/15	6 p.m.	Reveille 6 A.M. Drew M.T. Stores and Rations. Had car spring taken down & greased. Inspected Amb. Cars of 48 Fd. Amb. with its C.O. Mended Magneto Brown in W. Shelay, & 2 prs more.	a.e.m
Doullens	27/8/15	11 p.m.	Reveille 5.30 A.M. Saw Workshop Unit & Sanitary Section leave at 11 under M.S.S. & Doullens. Started with Amb. Cars at 2 p.m. arrived at 6 p.m. Distributed cars to its 3 sections.	a.e.m

Army Form C. 2118

WAR DIARY

~~INTELLIGENCE SUMMARY~~

(Erase heading not required.)

Instructions regarding War Diaries and Intelligence Summaries are contained in F. S. Regs., Part II. and the Staff Manual respectively. Title Pages will be prepared in manuscript.

Place	Date	Hour	Summary of Events and Information	Remarks and references to Appendices
Doullens	28/8/15	6.p.m	Reveille 5.30. Thoroughly cleaned Workshop lorries. Billets allotted & installed for heavy cars. Searched Doullens & found suitable place in main Arras Road. Borrowed sand bags.	O.C.M.
Doullens	29/8/15	6.p.m	Reveille 6.AM. Inspected sections, cars very dirty ordered cars to be redeaned, differently in future water. Received 4 tyres & 6 inner tubes. Made 4 wash troughs, 2 pails & uniform for A.D.M.S. Took return to Div. H.Q.	O.C.M.
Doullens	30/8/15	6.p.m	Reveille 6.AM. Inspected cars & passed them as clean. Repaired Ford Trailer. Took 8mm Wednesday main tackarle heavy cap to Skenn of fellow teddy picked. Wires for new ball bearing.	O.C.M
Doullens	31/8/15	6.p.m	Reveille 6.AM. Started moving side curtain for car. Issued covers for log books. Altered 160 patterns for 37 Div Infantry Co. Drew maps of Beauval & looked for a place for Workshop Unit at Var.	O.C.M

1875 Wt. W593/826 1,000,000 4/15 J.B.C. & A. A.D.S.S./Forms/C. 2118.

Army Form C. 2118

WAR DIARY
~~INTELLIGENCE SUMMARY~~

(Erase heading not required.)

Duplicate to late
"in place of Original
Sine actis"
transit

August 1915

3 Y Div 7 A.W.U.

O.C. Mackay Lieut

(Volume 1)

Instructions regarding War Diaries and Intelligence Summaries are contained in F. S. Regs., Part II. and the Staff Manual respectively. Title Pages will be prepared in manuscript.

Place	Date	Hour	Summary of Events and Information	Remarks and references to Appendices

Army Form C. 2118

WAR DIARY

~~INTELLIGENCE SUMMARY~~

(Erase heading not required.)

Instructions regarding War Diaries and Intelligence Summaries are contained in F. S. Regs., Part II. and the Staff Manual respectively. Title Pages will be prepared in manuscript.

Place	Date	Hour	Summary of Events and Information	Remarks and references to Appendices
	1915			
ROUEN	Aug 1	6 am.	Reveille 6 a.m. Drew stores from Ordnance Depot to complete equipment of personnel; also petrol, oil &c for 200 miles trek from M.T. Depot. Saw A.D.T and Base Commandant. Received orders.	Q.Q.M.
NEUFCHATEL	" 2	6 am.	Reveille 6 a.m. Drew coal from collier at Rouen & paid N.C.O. Left Rouen for NEUFCHATEL at 2 pm arriving there at 6 pm and staying overnight.	Q.C.M.
ABBEVILLE	" 3	6 pm.	Reveille 5 pm. Attached ambulance cars and Workshop to 34th Div Ammunition Column and left for ABBEVILLE at 7 a.m. Went on ahead with Major Commanding Col to ABBEVILLE, saw Base Commandant and received orders. Arranged to camp there for the night. Picked Column & brought into camp. Discovered faulty type on Workshop. Tried to change it with another Peerless at the Depot but wheels not being interchangeable had to replace.	Q.C.M.

Army Form C. 2118

WAR DIARY
~~INTELLIGENCE SUMMARY~~

(Erase heading not required.)

Instructions regarding War Diaries and Intelligence Summaries are contained in F.S. Regs., Part II. and the Staff Manual respectively. Title Pages will be prepared in manuscript.

Place	Date	Hour	Summary of Events and Information	Remarks and references to Appendices
	1915			
MOULLE	Aug 4	9 p.m.	Reveille 5 a.m. Left ABBEVILLE at 4 a.m. Found well FOS ambulance on a long hill. Outside FRUGES discovered that the Workshop had stripped a rear tyre. Proceeded to FRUGES and found that the remaining tyre of the wheel had also stripped. Telephoned A.D.T. ABBEVILLE and was instructed to 'phone ST OMER. D.O.T. sent out breakdown lorry with tyres which arrived at 6 p.m. Went into ST OMER and reported and arranged with Depot to let me have three tyres off another Peerless. Got convoy to MOULLE and found Div. has left. Went into ST OMER and got orders from O/C Troops	A C.u.
EECKE	Aug 5		Reveille 5 a.m. Reported to D.A.Q.M.G. at RENESCURE at 5.30 a.m. who promised to send orders later. Drew petrol & rations at ST OMER. Collected column and gave orders to have the cars thoroughly cleaned. Got no orders; no followers. DIVISION. HAZEBROUCK	A C.u.

Army Form C. 2118

WAR DIARY

INTELLIGENCE SUMMARY

(Erase heading not required.)

Instructions regarding War Diaries and Intelligence Summaries are contained in F.S. Regs., Part II. and the Staff Manual respectively. Title Pages will be prepared in manuscript.

Place	Date	Hour	Summary of Events and Information	Remarks and references to Appendices
EECKE (continued)	1915 Aug 5		Went on as I passed A.D.2.M.S. who gave me orders. Left 7 cars at 50th Field Ambulance HAZEBROUCK. Left 7 cars with 49th Field Ambulance at ST. SYLVESTRE. Took remainder and workshop to EECKE. Dark on arrival. So billets for the night in a yard with a firm bottom.	A. Orr
HAZEBROUCK	Aug 6	6 p.m. Reveille 6 a.m.	Orders to join 4 & 8th Field Ambulances. Handed over 7 ambulance cars. Found the place all over for the workshop was a farm yard without a solid bottom and with a very narrow approach road. Applies to A.D.M.S. to move back to HAZEBROUCK where I obtained a fine yard with concrete bottom. Also near Railhead to collect stores. Ambulance cars at 4 & 8th F.A. inspected by A.D.M.S. who ordered numerous structural alterations etc.	A. Orr

WAR DIARY

INTELLIGENCE SUMMARY

(Erase heading not required.)

Army Form C. 2118

Place	Date	Hour	Summary of Events and Information	Remarks and references to Appendices
HAZEBROUCK	1915 Aug 7	Reveille 6 am 6 pm	Started alterations to ambulances and Fords. Saw Ordnance Officer at CAESTRE and far Rin to arrange for service colour paint.	O.C. in
"	8	Reveille 6 am 6 pm	Called on O/C 49th and 50th Field Ambulances for more Wolseley alteration. Continues the type of Peerless Workshop again strip	O.C. in
"	9	Reveille 6 am 6 pm	Continues alterations to Wolseley. Went to EECKE to O/C 48th F.A. for more cars to be sent. Arranges to pick up mail bag at Railleas	O.C. in
"	10	Reveille 6 am 6 pm	Continues structural alterations to ambulance cars. Went to VILLIERS & purchased filling for the canvas sides of the cars. Total expenditure 33 francs. Went to ISBERGUES and left Workshop lorry. Called later and found that they required the wheel. Ordered wheel to be sent tomorrow.	O.C. in

Army Form C. 2118

WAR DIARY
INTELLIGENCE SUMMARY
(Erase heading not required.)

Place	Date	Hour	Summary of Events and Information	Remarks and references to Appendices
	1915			
HAZEBROUCK	Aug 11	Reveille 6 am	Continues alterations to Ambulance car. Called at ISBERGUES and picked up Peerless Workshop wheel & tyres	A.C.in
"	" 12	6 pm	Repairs two Fords with worn brake shoes & series for cellulois windows (for Fords) which were constantly being broken. Repairs 3 headlights	A.C.in
"	" 13	6 pm	Inspects cars of 48th 49th & 50th F.A.s. Repairs Ford Ambulance — damaged radiator and headlights. Starts making metal cap rope-hooks for 3 yr. Div Supply Column. Repairs Triumph motor cycle.	A.C.in
"	" 14	6 pm	Went to DIN H.Q. with awards Ford with awards radiator repaired and returned. Douglas motor bicycle repaired.	A.C.in
"	" 15	6 pm	Went to EECKE to bring in damaged Ford Ambulance which had to be towed by lorry. Examines damage. Starts repair.	A.C.in

1875   Wt. W593/826   1,000,000   4/15   J.B.C. & A.   A.D.S.S./Forms/C. 2118.

Army Form C. 2118.

WAR DIARY
INTELLIGENCE SUMMARY
(Erase heading not required.)

Instructions regarding War Diaries and Intelligence Summaries are contained in F. S. Regs., Part II. and the Staff Manual respectively. Title Pages will be prepared in manuscript.

Place	Date	Hour	Summary of Events and Information	Remarks and references to Appendices
	1915			
HAZEBROUCK	Aug 16	6am	Reveille 6 am	
		6pm	Went to Advanced M.T. Depot. ABBEVILLE to vans urgent stores. Was not allowed to draw them without services in. Left indent.	A.a.m.
"	" 17	6pm	Do	
			Was in workshop with broken steering arm. Searches round & purchased gas piping to replace arm cost 2.80.	A.a.m
"	" 18	6pm	Do	
			Inspected ambulance cars at various points No 2 Workshop towed in with sheared castellad. ions of rear M6 hub. Saw D.A.D.O.S. re Brodie Helmets	A.a.m.
"	" 19	6pm	Do	
			Went to Dis N.L., Drew cash, paid N.C.O. and men. Saw D.A.D.O.S. re needs for workshop & bought back service paint.	A.a.m.
"	" 20	6pm	Do	
			Went to STEENBECQUE and bought sheet iron $74.50 Started painting ambulance cars green.	A.a.m.

Army Form C. 2118

WAR DIARY
INTELLIGENCE SUMMARY

(Erase heading not required.)

Instructions regarding War Diaries and Intelligence Summaries are contained in F. S. Regs., Part II. and the Staff Manual respectively. Title Pages will be prepared in manuscript.

Place	Date	Hour	Summary of Events and Information	Remarks and references to Appendices
HAZEBROUCK	1915 Aug 21	6 pm	Painted 6 more Ambulance cars & stencilled identification marks. Received complaint re weakness of Wolseley spring	A.C.in
"	" 22	6 pm	Started experimenting on Wolseley No 15. Took down spring, cleaned them & prepared spring steel for extra leaf	
"	" 23	6 pm	Fitted up springs of Wolseley with extra leaf & overhauled the car & took it for a test run. Experiment proves very satisfactory.	A.C.in
"	" 24	6 pm	Arranges to have all oes Wolseley back in workshop to strengthen springs. Repairs magnets of No 2 Wolseley. Painted interiors of three cars white. Bought spring steel cost Fr 38.	A.C.in
"	" 25	6 pm	Repairs cars. Continued repairs to oes Wolseley & painted their interiors white. Inspected sections. Received orders to trek.	A.C.in

WAR DIARY

Army Form C. 2118

(Erase heading not required.)

Place	Date	Hour	Summary of Events and Information	Remarks and references to Appendices
HAZEBROUCK	1915 Aug 26	6 am	Reveille 6 am. Finished straightening spring of two old ambulances. Repaired supports for two canvas tops. Arranged for drawing rations near Hd. Div. HdQuarters. New m.t. stores at Railhead. Has touring car front spring taken down & greased. Went to EECKE and inspected cars with O/C. Found one magneto brush broken & one Ford brake worn out.	A.E.W.
DOULLENS	" 27	6 pm	Reveille 6 am Sent workshop, store van and Daimler lorry of Div Sanitary section on trek to DOULLENS at 8.30 am. Cleaned yards and left with 14 ambulance cars at 2 pm for DOULLENS. Arrived there at 6 pm and distributed Sections.	L.E.W.
"	" 28	6 pm	Reveille 6 am Searched DOULLENS for billets & Bivouacs in Annex road & found gas pipes for workshop	A.E.W.
"	" 29	6 pm	Reveille 6 am Made washing boards for A.D.M.S. and D.H.Q. Inspected section cars at ORVILLE	A.E.W.

Army Form C. 2118

WAR DIARY
or
INTELLIGENCE SUMMARY
(Erase heading not required.)

Instructions regarding War Diaries and Intelligence Summaries are contained in F.S. Regs., Part II. and the Staff Manual respectively. Title Pages will be prepared in manuscript.

Place	Date	Hour	Summary of Events and Information	Remarks and references to Appendices
DOULLENS	1915 Aug 30	6am	Reveille 6am made Log Book holders for 34th Div Supply Col and rope hooks for their lorries. Unloaded 4 tons	Officer
"	" 31	6am	Reveille 6am Inspected Section cars at Halloy made case for O/c 50th Field Ambulance.	Officer

1875 Wt. W593/826 1,000,000 4/15 J.B.C. & A. A.D.S.S./Forms/C. 2118.

WAR DIARY

Army Form C. 2118

September
October 1915

37° Div. T. A.W.U.

G.S. Mackay
Lieut

WAR DIARY
INTELLIGENCE SUMMARY
(Erase heading not required.)

Army Form C. 2118

Instructions regarding War Diaries and Intelligence Summaries are contained in F.S. Regs., Part II. and the Staff Manual respectively. Title Pages will be prepared in manuscript.

Place	Date	Hour	Summary of Events and Information	Remarks and references to Appendices
Doullens	1915 Oct 1st	6 p.m.	Reveille 6 A.M. Inspected section Amy. Cars at Mondicourt. No. 7 installing with broken funnel leaking in wrong gear.	O.C.in
--	2nd	6 p.m.	Reveille 6 a.m. Made Day book hours for 37 Div. S.Cn. also A.D.M.S.	O.C.in
--	3rd	6 p.m.	--	Started washing section. Inspected section at 4 a.m. cars dirty orderd cleaned to condition inished. No I working	O.C.in
--	4"	6 p.m.	--	units fander magnets. No I whiteley magnets action in.	O.C.in
Doullens	5"	6 p.m.	--	Fresh magnets. Received orders to Par a selected	O.C.in
Par.	6"	6 p.m.	Reveille 4:30 A.M. Moved to Par. Took over billets & fed day.	O.C.in
--	7"	6 p.m.	Reveille 6 A.m. Searched & found truck + wagon for cleaning cars + cleaned out billet cesspool	O.C.in
--	8"	6 p.m.	--	Improved horses + cleaned out billet cesspool; made 3 p.m. boards for various Div. Offices	O.C.in
--	9"	6 p.m.	--	Made stretcher carriers for 49' Fed. Amv. went to Doullens & bought hinges for them. Hr. 50.	O.C.in

WAR DIARY

Army Form C. 2118

(Erase heading not required.)

Place	Date 1915 Sept.	Hour	Summary of Events and Information	Remarks and references to Appendices
Pas	10	6 p.m.	Reveille 6 A.M. Inspected Amb. Section at Humber champ. Made them start cleaning their cars over again. Sent to No. 15 Fd. Ambn. taken down & cleaned & returned. Started 3 cylinder taking in old outer covers, inflations, & using again in making car in with broken motion. Made a new end to a convoy as D.A.D.O.S. refused to supply one.	O.C. ...
—	11	6 p.m.	Started a weekly inspection of all Amb. cars to let us know today light & nuts. Found several loose.	O.C. ...
—	12	6 p.m.	U. W.M.S. today. Made Stretchers for made driven lights then. Made an estimate for the trench miners a game on an estimate for 12 special boards to the Div.	O.C. ...
—	13	6 p.m.	Started batteries for the Div. Also made lathe blades. Seven 1"x2" for the Separators. Started lathery and key for lifting sluice gates.	O.C. ...
—	14	6 p.m.	Continued baths & inflations. Made weekly hooks for 7th Amb. Sent them a despatch carrier window frames.	O.C. ...
—	15	6 p.m.	Carried in with baths & windows frames. Overhauled & cleaned two Ford cars.	O.C. ...

WAR DIARY

(Erase heading not required.)

Army Form C. 2118

Place	Date	Hour	Summary of Events and Information	Remarks and references to Appendices
Pas	1915 Sept 16th	6 p.m.	Reveille 6 AM. Went to Amiens bought material for extra drive from engine for Dynamo. Overhauled & cleaned his Ford. Inspected C of E workshops. Bought material for watch houses etc.	O. C. Cav.
—	17	6 p.m.	Went to Amiens - collected yesterday's purchases. Proceeded to Meriveux - paid men. Overhauled & cleaned 2 Fords. Started making watch houses.	O. C. Cav.
—	18	6 p.m.	Finished baths etc. to Trench houses. Overhauled & cleaned engine No. 1 workshop. Inspected section Vulcanizing b lathe & lorries of 3rd Div. & Hans. S. Cn.	O. C. Cav.
—	19	6 p.m.	Repaired spring No. 1 W Staley. Inspected section & Vas. Vulcanizing & new tyres. Repaired 3rd Div. R.F.A. Hq. Sunbeam car.	O. C. Cav.
—	20	6 p.m.	Inspected all sections Amt. Cav. for lorries U. W. G. body trucks etc. Went on to Bienvillers & established a workshop and anger in etc. Bro. J.W. Gas on for 49th Fd. Amb. in Bellevue.	O. C. Cav.

1875 Wt. W593/826 4/15 1,000,000 J.B.C. & A. A.D.S.S./Forms/C. 2118.

WAR DIARY

INTELLIGENCE SUMMARY

(Erase heading not required.)

Army Form C. 2118

Place	Date	Hour	Summary of Events and Information	Remarks and references to Appendices
Par.	1915 21.	6 p.m.	Reveille 6 A.M. 49 7th Can. sent in for 4 tent windows frames & sashes. Went to Dundas Major with Q. Br. shops for steam. Overhauled & cleaned engine No. 15 & sundry work. Made an acetylene lamp for D.H.Q. is light.	A. Cuy.
—	22	6 p.m.	Started painting spare wheels. Went to Annois [illegible] camp for R.E.	A. Cuy.
—	23	6 p.m.	Made lamps for R.E. and 2 & gate. Retail bins. Overhauled & cleaned wheeler engine. Sent light lorry to D.H.Q. Painted 4 Amb. cars & 3 Rolls Horse carts.	A. Cuy.
—	24	6 p.m.	Painted 6 Amb. Cars & 2 Cav. Horse carts. Also made 36 detachable Rods &c for S. wagon. D.H.Q. Daimler sent in for repair. [illegible] car all cleared up.	A. Cuy.
—	25	6 p.m.	Inspected & sorted Amb. Cars. Did sundry work for R.E. Carried on Repair to Daimler car.	A. Cuy.
—	26	6 p.m.	Delivered 12 pairs stretcher carriers to 49 Feilden. Painted moving made own for 48 7th Amb. Saw D.D.S.&T. re permission to go to M.T. Abbeyville	A. Cuy.

Army Form C. 2118

WAR DIARY

~~XXXXXXXXX XXXXXXX~~

(Erase heading not required.)

Instructions regarding War Diaries and Intelligence Summaries are contained in F. S. Regs., Part II. and the Staff Manual respectively. Title Pages will be prepared in manuscript.

Place	Date	Hour	Summary of Events and Information	Remarks and references to Appendices
Pas	1918 27	6 p.m.	Reveille 6 a.m. Went to Ablainville & drew fresh traversing rollers. (two) having sent ours in to be Vulcanized, the others made into spares. 8 hours service for R.E.	A.Coy
--	28	6 p.m.	Reveille 6 a.m. Repaired Davidson lorry, Sanitary Section, hauled their latrine shed. Inspected Pas Quil. Section. Wellington Sparkler by Arms. Put up 20 signs on Div. area.	A.Coy
--	29	6 p.m.	Reveille 6 a.m. Repaired trailer, lorries, car.	A.Coy
--	30	6 p.m.	Reveille 6 a.m. Repaired Ford Van. Axle finished old one was a bad welder. 9 hours work for R.E.	A.Coy

1875 Wt. W593/826 1,000,000 4/15 J.B.C. & A. A.D.S.S./Forms/C. 2118.

12/7430

37th Brig: F.a.W. Units
vol 3

Oct 15

WAR DIARY

INTELLIGENCE SUMMARY

October 1915

34th Div. F.A.W.U.

C.C. Mackay
Lieut.

Volume 3

Army Form C. 2118

WAR DIARY

~~INTELLIGENCE SUMMARY~~

(Erase heading not required.)

Instructions regarding War Diaries and Intelligence Summaries are contained in F. S. Regs., Part II. and the Staff Manual respectively. Title Pages will be prepared in manuscript.

Place	Date	Hour	Summary of Events and Information	Remarks and references to Appendices
Pos	1915 Oct. 1st	6 pm	Reveille 6 am. Went to Amiens & purchased lamps to light Divisional Baths finishing. Started making trailer to attach to light lorry to carry surplus timber etc.	O.C. m
"	2	6 pm	Reveille 6 am. Carried on with trailer. Started making cane firing to attack to light lorry to permit of use of back of lorry.	O.C. m
"	3	6 pm	Reveille 6 am. Started painting out all identification marks on Ambulance cars. Carried on with trailer and light lorry crane	O.C. m
"	4	6 pm	Reveille 6 am. Started making 16 lamps for artillery out of 4 gallon petrol tins. Went 16 see D.D.S.T.	O.C. m
"	5	6 pm	Reveille 6 am. Inspected sections. Repaired Douglas moto cycle for 34th Divl Supply Column. Repaired Douglas moto cycle of 4.9th Field Ambulance Repaired Triumph moto cycle of 50th Field Ambulance	O.C. m

1875 Wt. W593/826 1,000,000 4/15 J.B.C. & A. A.D.S.S./Form/C. 2118.

Army Form C. 2118

WAR DIARY

INTELLIGENCE SUMMARY
(Erase heading not required.)

Instructions regarding War Diaries and Intelligence Summaries are contained in F.S. Regs., Part II. and the Staff Manual respectively. Title Pages will be prepared in manuscript.

Place	Date	Hour	Summary of Events and Information	Remarks and references to Appendices
P.A.S.	1915 Oct 6	6pm	Reveille 6am. Started repairs on another Douglas motor cycle for the 3/c Div Supply Column.	O.C.M.
"	7th	6pm	Reveille 6am. Repaired O.C.'s two gentles. Petrol engine for the Royal Engineers. Tried new magneto on the R.E's petrol engine. Connected and sent out to Royal Engineers. Started making insulators for Signallers.	O.C.M.
"	8	6pm	Reveille 6am. Moved new bicycles & cleaned out the new one. Started repairs to bodywork of Wolseley Ambulance.	O.C.M.
"	9	6pm	Reveille 6am. Went to Doullens & bought glass for windows. Made frames & sent out to 49th Field Ambulance. Inspected No 2 Section.	O.C.M.
"	10	6pm	Reveille 6am. Received supply of electric starters. Bought fasteners in Amiens to replace for windows to broken celluloid.	O.C.M.
"	11	6pm	Reveille 6am. Inspected No 1 Section. For loose bolts &c. Found awac brake linings worn.	O.C.M.

Army Form C. 2118

WAR DIARY
INTELLIGENCE SUMMARY
(Erase heading not required.)

Instructions regarding War Diaries and Intelligence Summaries are contained in F. S. Regs., Part II. and the Staff Manual respectively. Title Pages will be prepared in manuscript.

Place	Date	Hour	Summary of Events and Information	Remarks and references to Appendices
PAS	1915 Oct 12	6pm	Reveille 6am. Repairs cloth of Wolseley light lorry; altered tarpaulin cover ring; made & fitted extra roof supports	O.C.m.
"	" 13	6pm	Reveille 6am. Tones in broken down Wolseley Ambulance from near Amiens. Found near hub key sheared wires for new hub made less for Wolseley light lorry. Inspected no 2 section car for loose bolts &c.	O.C.m.
"	14	6pm	Reveille 6am. Took down & cleaned motor cycle of no 3 section. Received 6 more motor cycles. Painted signs on all ambulances; took off Divisional mark. Inspected no 3 section.	O.C.m.
"	15	6pm	Reveille 6am. Repairs tyres & tubes up new motor cycles as made them ready for delivery to the sections. Found magnetos faulty, owing apparently to wet getting inside during transit.	O.C.m.
"	16	6pm	Reveille 6am. Self drives to Dier Hospital workshop carries on &, Mechanic Staff Sergeant	O.C.m.

WAR DIARY

Army Form C. 2118

(Erase heading not required.)

Place	Date	Hour	Summary of Events and Information	Remarks and references to Appendices
PAS	1915 Oct-14	6pm	Reveille bar. Overhauled Walsely ambulance No 15. Made chimney piping for 48th Field Ambulance.	O.C.rm
"	16	6pm	Went to Doullens & bought strip iron for A.D.M.S. to make rest shelters traverses. Made a pattern. Overhauled Douglas motor cycle.	O.C.rm
"	19	6pm	Started making shelter traverses, turns out 100. Bought laid wood for car top. Made new joints for R.E.s.	O.C.rm
"	20	6pm	Turned out 100 traverses for shelters. Went to Ypres to see new bomb machine for the Engineers. Sent lorry for large wooden axle.	O.C.rm
"	21	6pm	Turned out another 100 traverses. Took down Walseley ambulance & cleaned as required. Overhauled Screwed piping for R.E.s.	O.C.rm

Army Form C. 2118

WAR DIARY

~~INTELLIGENCE SUMMARY~~

(Erase heading not required.)

Instructions regarding War Diaries and Intelligence Summaries are contained in F.S. Regs., Part II. and the Staff Manual respectively. Title Pages will be prepared in manuscript.

Place	Date	Hour	Summary of Events and Information	Remarks and references to Appendices
P.A.S.	1915 Oct 22	6pm	Turned out 120 trousers to complete Reservables Walseley ambulance. Douglas motor cycle received from Div Supply Col for repair. Cleaned Triumph motor cycle for 50th F.A.	O.C. in
"	" 23	6pm	Went to Amiens & bought circular saw for Royal Engineers. Purchased two Walseley ambulances. Started making body for Walseley car. Started stone fitting for North Staffords	O.C. in
"	" 24	6pm	Made two baths – one for Div supply Col & one for Foyae North Lancs. Finished two Walseley ambulances. Started fitted cap improvements for motor cycles	O.C. in
"	" 25	6pm	Went to Amiens & bought shafting for circular saw to be erected for R.E. Continues making body for Walseley Repairs Douglas motor cycle Tested Douglas motor cycle	Q.C. in

A.D.S.S./Forms/C. 21185.

WAR DIARY

INTELLIGENCE SUMMARY

(Erase heading not required.)

Army Form C. 2118

Place	Date	Hour	Summary of Events and Information	Remarks and references to Appendices
PAS.	1915 Oct 26	6pm	Reveille 6 am. Inspected no 3 Section & arranges to make brick standing for cars. Received fitters coal kits. Overhauls Motor Cy No 1.	O.C.W.
"	" 27	6pm	Repaired motor cycle. Dismantled & repaired magnets of new Douglas motor cycle. Overhauls Ford Ambulance & took up bearings	C.R.M.
"	" 28	6pm	Inspected no 2 Section. Started making new steps for Fords. Lathe work for C.R.E.	O.C.M.
"	" 29	6pm	Ditto. new steps to 3 Fords. Continued lathe work for C.R.E. Went to Division ad Beste to superintend erection of SC. officing	O.C. in
"	" 30	6pm	Repaired water cart. Made 3 stands. Started making Sterilizer for 4.8.R. Fd Amb.	O.C.M.

WAR DIARY

INTELLIGENCE SUMMARY

(Erase heading not required.)

Army Form C. 2118

Place	Date	Hour	Summary of Events and Information	Remarks and references to Appendices
PAS	1915 Oct 31	6 pm	Reveille 6 am. Went to Humber camp & inspected section. Repaired late windows. Fitted up stove for C.R.E. Gave men half holiday	O.C. yr [Maz]

37th F.A.U.
tot: 4

121/7604

Om 23

37th Bhram

Nov 15

WAR DIARY
of
INTELLIGENCE SUMMARY
(Erase heading not required.)

Army Form C.2118

Instructions regarding War Diaries and Intelligence Summaries are contained in F.S. Regs., Part II. and the Staff Manual respectively. Title Pages will be prepared in manuscript.

CONFIDENTIAL

WAR DIARY
— of —

A.C. MACKAY 2ND LIEUT

COMMANDING - 37 DIV. F.A.W.U.

From 1st Nov. 1915 to 30th Nov. 1915

(VOLUME 4)

Army Form C. 2

WAR DIARY
or
INTELLIGENCE SUMMARY

(Erase heading not required.)

Instructions regarding War Diaries and Intelligence Summaries are contained in F. S. Regs., Part II. and the Staff Manual respectively. Title Pages will be prepared in manuscript.

Place	Date	Hour	Summary of Events and Information	Remarks and references to Appendices
PAS	Nov.1.	6 P.M.	Reveille 6 A.M. Carried on with the usual workshops routine. Completed a stove for the Royal Engineers	O.C.w.
"	Nov.2	6 P.M.	Reveille 6 A.M. Carried on with the usual workshops routine	O.C.w.
"	Nov.3	6 P.M.	Reveille 6 A.M. Carried on with the usual workshops routine. Turned a number of wooden switch plugs for the Royal Engineers.	O.C.w.
"	Nov.4	6 P.M.	Reveille 6 A.M. Effected repairs to a steam valve for the Royal Engineers. Carried on with the usual workshops routine.	O.C.w.
"	Nov.5	6 P.M.	Reveille 6 A.M. Turned a number of exhaust valves for the Royal Engineers. Carried on with the usual workshops routine.	O.C.w.
"	Nov.6 to Nov.9	6 P.M.	Reveille 6 A.M. Carried on with the usual workshops routine.	O.C.w.
"	Nov 10	6 P.M.	Reveille 6 A.M. Made a number of lamp hangers for the 49th Field Ambulance. Carried on with the usual workshop routine.	O.C.w.

1875. Wt. W593/826 1,000,000 4/15 J.B.C. & A. A.D.S.S./Forms/C. 2118.

1.

WAR DIARY
INTELLIGENCE SUMMARY
(Erase heading not required.)

Army Form C. 2

Instructions regarding War Diaries and Intelligence Summaries are contained in F.S. Regs., Part II. and the Staff Manual respectively. Title Pages will be prepared in manuscript.

Place	Date	Hour	Summary of Events and Information	Remarks and references to Appendices
PAS.	Nov.11 to Nov.12	6 P.M. 6 P.M.	Reveille 6 A.M. Carried on with the usual workshop routine.	O.C.W.
"	Nov.13	6 P.M.	Reveille 6 A.M. Effected repairs to threshing machine attached to A.S.C. 110 Brigade. Carried on with the usual workshop routine.	O.C.W.
"	Nov.14	6 P.M.	Reveille 6 A.M. Made a quantity of terminals and washers for the Royal Engineers. Carried on with the usual workshop routine.	O.C.W.
"	Nov.15 to Nov.17	6 P.M. 6 P.M.	Reveille 6 A.M. Carried on with the usual workshop routine.	O.C.W.
"	Nov.18	6 P.M.	Reveille 6 A.M. Received a message stating that a Ford Ambulance was in difficulties on the road between HUMBERCAMPS and POMMIER owing to having been in collision with another Ambulance Car. Sent out a breakdown party with the 30 cwt Lorry and had the Ford towed to the workshops for repair. Carried on with the usual workshop routine.	O.C.W.

2.

Army Form C.2

WAR DIARY or INTELLIGENCE SUMMARY

(Erase heading not required.)

Instructions regarding War Diaries and Intelligence Summaries are contained in F. S. Regs., Part II. and the Staff Manual respectively. Title Pages will be prepared in manuscript.

Place	Date	Hour	Summary of Events and Information	Remarks and references to Appendices
PAS.	Nov.19 to Nov.20	6 P.M. 6 P.M.	Reveille 6 A.M. Carried on with the usual workshops routine.	O.C.m
"	Nov 21	6 P.M.	Reveille 6 A.M. Received a message stating that a Wolseley Ambulance had obtained a breakdown on the road between POMMIER and BERLES-AU-BOIS, and was unable to proceed. Sent out a breakdown party with the 30 cwt Lorry and had the Ambulance Car towed to the workshops for repair. Carried on with the usual workshops routine. Started to make 500 Iron French Scrapers for the Royal Engineers.	O.C.m
"	Nov.22 to Nov.28	6 P.M. 6 P.M.	Reveille 6 A.M. Carried on with the usual workshops routine.	O.C.m
"	Nov 29	6 P.M.	Reveille 6 A.M. Workshops inspected by G.O.C. Carried on with the usual workshops routine.	O.C.m
	Nov 30	6 P.M.	Reveille 6 A.M. Carried on with the usual workshops routine. Received a request to tow in a Ford Car belonging to the B.R.C.S. which was in difficulties on the HENU Road. Sent out the 30 cwt Lorry & had the Car towed to the workshops.	O.C.m

3.

Army Form C. 2118

WAR DIARY
or
INTELLIGENCE SUMMARY
(Erase heading not required.)

Instructions regarding War Diaries and Intelligence Summaries are contained in F.S. Regs., Part II. and the Staff Manual respectively. Title Pages will be prepared in manuscript.

Place	Date	Hour	Summary of Events and Information	Remarks and references to Appendices

1875 Wt. W593/826 1,000,000 4/15 J.B.C. & A. A.D.S.S./Forms/C. 2118.

37th F.A.U.U.
vol: #5

37th Braun

December 1918

Army Form C. 2118

WAR DIARY
~or~
INTELLIGENCE SUMMARY
(Erase heading not required.)

Lieut. A.E. Mackay
O/c 34th Div. F.A. W.U.

Dec 1915

(Volume V)

Army Form C. 2118

WAR DIARY
or
INTELLIGENCE SUMMARY

(Erase heading not required.)

Instructions regarding War Diaries and Intelligence Summaries are contained in F. S. Regs., Part II. and the Staff Manual respectively. Title Pages will be prepared in manuscript.

Place	Date	Hour	Summary of Events and Information	Remarks and references to Appendices
P.A.S.	1915 Dec 1	6 am 6 pm	Reveille Carried on usual Workshop Routine Continued making Trench scrapers for R.E.s and fitting up new auxiliary drive for workshop Generator	A.C.J...
"	Dec 2	6 pm	Carried on usual workshop Routine	A.C...
"	Dec 3	6 pm	Carried on usual workshop Routine	A.C...
"	" 4	6 pm	Started making & fitting side doors to No 13 Ford ambulance.	A.C...
"	" 5	6 pm	Carried on usual workshop Routine Root foot plates & steering of No 5 Ford	A.C...
"	" 6	6 pm	Carried on usual workshop Routine	A.C...
"	" 7	6 pm	Fitted new side doors to No 19 Ford	A.C...
"	" 8	6 pm	Carried on usual workshop Routine	A.C...

1875 Wt. W593/826 1,000,000 4/15 J.B.C. & A. A.D.S.S./Forms/C. 2118.

Army Form C. 2118

WAR DIARY
or
INTELLIGENCE SUMMARY
(Erase heading not required.)

Instructions regarding War Diaries and Intelligence Summaries are contained in F. S. Regs., Part II. and the Staff Manual respectively. Title Pages will be prepared in manuscript.

Place	Date	Hour	Summary of Events and Information	Remarks and references to Appendices
PAS	1915 Dec 9	6 pm	Reveille 6 am. Started making new design of machine gun mounting for 16th Batt. M.M.G.S. Fitted side door to No 6 Ford	A.O.C.
"	" 10	"	Carried on usual workshop Routine	O.C.
"	" 11	"	"	"
"	" 12	"	Overhauled No 5 Ford	"
"	" 13	"	Carried on usual Workshop Routine	A.O.C.
"	" 14	"	"	"
"	" 15	"	Repaired Douglas motor cycle for No 1 Section. Started repairing stretcher carrier for 49th F.A.	O.C.
"	" 16	"	Carried on usual workshop Routine	O.C.
"	" 17	"	"	"
"	" 18	"	"	O.C.

1875 Wt. W593/826 1,000,000 4/15 J.B.C. & A. A.D.S.S./Forms/C. 2118.

WAR DIARY
or
INTELLIGENCE SUMMARY
(Erase heading not required.)

Army Form C. 2118

Place	Date	Hour	Summary of Events and Information	Remarks and references to Appendices
PAS	1915 Dec 19	6pm	Reveille 6 am Carried out alterations to petrol engine & Water wheel for Divisional Baths.	A.e.m
"	" 20	"	Carried on usual workshop Routine	A.e.m
"	" 21	"	" " "	A.e.m
"	" 22	"	Fitted Side Door to No 16 Wolseley, made & fitted windscreen	A.e.m
"	" 23	"	Carried on usual workshop Routine	A.e.m
"	" 24	"	" " " "	"
"	" 25	"	" " " "	"
"	" 26	"	Made & fitted new windscreen to No 9 Wolseley	A.e.m
"	" 27	"	Fitted new side doors & windscreen to No 15 Wolseley & overhauled engine	A.e.m
"	" 28	"	Carried on usual workshop Routine	

Army Form C. 2118

WAR DIARY
or
INTELLIGENCE SUMMARY
(Erase heading not required.)

Instructions regarding War Diaries and Intelligence Summaries are contained in F. S. Regs., Part II. and the Staff Manual respectively. Title Pages will be prepared in manuscript.

Place	Date	Hour	Summary of Events and Information	Remarks and references to Appendices
PAS	1915 Dec 29	6 p	Reveille 6 am carries on usual workshop Routine	O.C.
"	" 30	"	" " Fitted side doors to No 4 Jos	O.C.
"	" 31	"	" " carries on usual workshop Routine	O.C.

1875 Wt. W593/826 1,000,000 4/15 J.B.C. & A. A.D.S.S./Forms/C. 2118.

Army Form C. 2118

WAR DIARY
or
INTELLIGENCE SUMMARY
(Erase heading not required.)

Summary of Events and Information

of

Lieut. FG Mackay
O/C 34th Div F.A.W.U.
For
JANUARY 1916

(VOLUME 6)
Confidential

Army Form C. 2118

WAR DIARY
INTELLIGENCE SUMMARY
(Erase heading not required.)

Instructions regarding War Diaries and Intelligence Summaries are contained in F. S. Regs., Part II. and the Staff Manual respectively. Title Pages will be prepared in manuscript.

Place	Date	Hour	Summary of Events and Information	Remarks and references to Appendices
PAS	1916 Jany 1	6 pm	Reveille 6.30 A.M. Carries on with usual Workshop Routine	A.P.M
"	" 2	"	" " " " " " " " "	
"	" 3	"	" " " " " " " " "	
"	" 4	"	" " " " " " " " "	
"	" 5	"	" " " " " " " " "	
"	" 6	"	Jones Napier Lorry from Jaudrempre and overhauled for 145 Coy R.Es	A.P.M
"	" 7	"	Carries on with usual Workshop Routine	A.P.M
"	" 8	"	" " " " " " " "	
"	" 9	"	" " " " " " " "	
"	" 10	"	Started making & painting 100 sign posts for 34th Div A.P.M.	A.P.M
"	" 11	"	" " " " " " " "	
"	" 12	"	Carries on with usual Workshop Routine	A.P.M
"	" 13	"	" " " " " " " "	

1875 Wt. W593/826 1,000,000 4/15 J.B.C. & A. A.D.S.S./Forms/C. 2118.

Army Form C. 2118

WAR DIARY
INTELLIGENCE SUMMARY
(Erase heading not required.)

Instructions regarding War Diaries and Intelligence Summaries are contained in F. S. Regs., Part II. and the Staff Manual respectively. Title Pages will be prepared in manuscript.

Place	Date	Hour	Summary of Events and Information	Remarks and references to Appendices
PAS	1916 Jany 14	6 p.m.	Reveille 6 A.M. Carries on with Naval Workshop Routine	O.C.in
"	" 15	"	" " " " " "	
"	" 16	"	" " " " " "	
"	" 17	"	" " " " " "	
"	" 18	"	" " " " " "	
"	" 19	"	" " " " " "	
"	" 20	"	Finishes making & painting 100 sign posts for 34th Div A.P.M.	O.C.in
"	" 21	"	Carries on Naval Workshop Routine. Starts improvements to interior of bodywork of Ford Ambulance car. Authority D.O.T. 4539 dated 14.1.16	O.C.in
"	" 22	"	Carries on Naval Workshop Routine	O.C.in
"	" 23	"	" " " " "	
"	" 24	"	" " " " "	
"	" 25	"	" " " " "	
"	" 26	"	" " " " "	

Army Form C. 2118

WAR DIARY

~~INTELLIGENCE SUMMARY~~

(Erase heading not required.)

Instructions regarding War Diaries and Intelligence Summaries are contained in F. S. Regs., Part II. and the Staff Manual respectively. Title Pages will be prepared in manuscript.

Place	Date	Hour	Summary of Events and Information	Remarks and references to Appendices
PAS	1916 Jany 27	6 p	Reveille 6 A.M. Carried on usual works &c Routine	O.C.us
"	" 28	"	" " " " "	
"	" 29	"	" " " " "	
"	" 30	"	" " " " "	
"	" 31	"	" " " " "	

34th Y.A.W.W.

Feb 1916

37th F.a.W.U.
Vol: 7

Army Form C. 2118.

WAR DIARY
~~INTELLIGENCE SUMMARY~~
(Erase heading not required.)

Instructions regarding War Diaries and Intelligence Summaries are contained in F. S. Regs., Part II. and the Staff Manual respectively. Title pages will be prepared in manuscript.

of
Lieut. J.C. Mackay
o/c 34th Div T.M.W.U.

FEBRUARY 1916
(VOLUME 1)

Place	Date	Hour	Summary of Events and Information	Remarks and references to Appendices

Army Form C. 2118.

WAR DIARY

~~INTELLIGENCE~~ SUMMARY

(Erase heading not required.)

Instructions regarding War Diaries and Intelligence Summaries are contained in F. S. Regs., Part II. and the Staff Manual respectively. Title pages will be prepared in manuscript.

Place	Date	Hour	Summary of Events and Information	Remarks and references to Appendices
	1916			
PAS	Feb 1	6 am	Reveille 6 am Carried on with usual Workshop Routine	Orders
"	" 2	6 pm	Continues alterations to interiors of Fords Ambulances.	Orders
"	" 3	6 pm	Carries on with usual Workshop Routine	
"	" 4	"	" " " " "	
"	" 5	"	" " " " "	
"	" 6	"	" " " " "	
"	" 7	"	" " " " "	
"	" 8	"	Provides lighting etc for Divisional Cinema Theatre	Orders
"	" 9	"	Carries on with usual Workshop Routine	
"	" 10	"	" " " " "	
"	" 11	"	" " " " "	

T2134. Wt. W708-776. 500000. 4/15. Sir J. C. & S.

Army Form C. 2118.

WAR DIARY
INTELLIGENCE SUMMARY
(Erase heading not required.)

Place	Date	Hour	Summary of Events and Information	Remarks and references to Appendices
	1916			
PAS	Feby 12	6 a.m.	Reveille 6 a.m. - Carries on Manual Workshop Routine	A.e.in
"	" 13	"	" " " "	A.e.in
			Towed in No 2 Wolseley which for the third time has sheared spring pinon off hub.	A.e.in
"	" 14	"	Carries on Manual Workshop Routine	A.e.in
"	" 15	"	" " " "	
"	" 16	"	" " " "	
"	" 17	"	" " " "	
"	" 18	"	Started preparations to trek to Bavincourt	A.e.in
"	" 19	"	Sent advance party to BAVINCOURT to prepare billets for N.C.Os men and yard for Workshop.	A.e.in
BAVINCOURT	" 20	"	Proceeded with Workshop to new quarters at Bavincourt	A.e.in
"	" 21	"	Towed in No 11 Wolseley with broken back axle casing	A.e.in

Army Form C. 2118.

WAR DIARY
INTELLIGENCE SUMMARY.
(Erase heading not required.)

Place	Date	Hour	Summary of Events and Information	Remarks and references to Appendices
	1916			
BAVINCOURT	FEB 22	6p	Reveille 6 am. Carries on usual Workshop Routine	O.C. in
"	"23	"	" " " " " "	"
"	"24	"	" " " " " "	"
			Started building garage for ambulances in Workshop for Repair	O.C. in
"	"25	"	Carries on usual Workshop Routine	O.C. in
"	"26	"	" " " "	"
"	"27	"	" " " "	"
"	"28	"	" " " "	"
			Saw No. 15 (60S type) Wolseley to A.S.C. Base ST OMER for repair as replacements were not available	O.C. in
"	"29	"	Carries on usual Workshop Routine. Sent two 20 H.p Studebaker box cars to A.S.C. Base Rouen for 16th Batty M.M.G.S.	O.C. in

3rd D.
F.A.W.U
Vol 8

March 1916

COMMITTEE FOR THE
MEDICAL HISTORY OF THE WAR
Date 9 - JUN '25

Army Form C. 2118.

WAR DIARY

INTELLIGENCE SUMMARY
(Erase heading not required.)

Lieut. A.C. Mackay
O/C 37th Div. 7. A. W. C.

MARCH 1916
(Volume 8)

Army Form C. 2118.

WAR DIARY
or
INTELLIGENCE SUMMARY.
(Erase heading not required.)

Instructions regarding War Diaries and Intelligence Summaries are contained in F. S. Regs., Part II. and the Staff Manual respectively. Title pages will be prepared in manuscript.

Place	Date	Hour	Summary of Events and Information	Remarks and references to Appendices
	1916			
BAVINCOURT	MAR 1	6 pm	Reveille 6 am Carries on usual workshop Routine	Appx
"	" 2	"	"	
"	" 3	"	"	
"	" 4	"	"	
"	" 5	"	"	
"	" 6	"	Started making machine gun flash protectors for Div H.Q. Carries on usual workshop Routine and alterations to interior of Ford Ambulance cars	Appx
"	" 7	"	"	
"	" 8	"	"	Appx
"	" 9	"	Carries on usual workshop Routine	
"	" 10	"	"	
"	" 11	"	"	Appx
"	" 12	"	"	
"	" 13	"	Losses in Wolseley Ambulance A15293 with broken rear axle casing	Appx

T2134. Wt. W708—776. 500000. 4/15. Sir J. C. & S.

Army Form C. 2118.

WAR DIARY
or
INTELLIGENCE SUMMARY.
(Erase heading not required.)

Instructions regarding War Diaries and Intelligence Summaries are contained in F. S. Regs., Part II. and the Staff Manual respectively. Title pages will be prepared in manuscript.

Place	Date	Hour	Summary of Events and Information	Remarks and references to Appendices
	1916			
BAVINCOURT	MAR/4	6 am	Reveille 6 am Carries on usual workshop Routine	Appx
"	" 15	"	" " " " " "	Appx
"	" 17	"	" " " " " "	Appx
"	" 18	"	Proceeds to LUCHIEUX to find suitable place for workshop during Divisional rest. Carries on usual workshop Routine	Appx
"	" 19	"	Starts packing up preparatory to moving off with Division	Appx
LUCHIEUX	" 20	"	Proceeds with workshop to Luchieux Sent two Wolseley cars to A.S.C. Base ST OMER	Appx
"	" 21	"		
"	" 22	"	Carries on usual workshop Routine	Appx
"	" 23	"	Starts overhauling and painting all Ambulance cars	Appx
"	" 24	"	Carries on usual workshop Routine	Appx
"	" 25	"	" " " " " "	
"	" 26	"	" " " " " "	

T2134. Wt. W708—776. 500000. 4/15. Sir J. C. & S.

Army Form C. 2118.

WAR DIARY
or
INTELLIGENCE SUMMARY.
(Erase heading not required.)

Instructions regarding War Diaries and Intelligence Summaries are contained in F. S. Regs., Part II. and the Staff Manual respectively. Title pages will be prepared in manuscript.

Place	Date	Hour	Summary of Events and Information	Remarks and references to Appendices
LUCHIEUX	1916 Mar 27	6 p.m	Reveille 6 am Carries on usual workshop Routine	actin
"	" 28	"	"	
"	" 29	"	"	actin
"	" 30	"	Took delivery of two Siddeley Deasy ambulances and one Wolseley to replace three cars previously sent to the 73 A S E Carries on usual workshop Routine	actin
"	" 31	"	"	actin
			Tours in No 17 Wolseley	

www.ingramcontent.com/pod-product-compliance
Lightning Source LLC
Chambersburg PA
CBHW081242170426
43191CB00034B/2012